MY JOURNEY TO THE THRONE

(and things I have learned along the way)

By

Judy Blanford

DEDICATION

This book is dedicated to Janie and Carolin, the two women God brought into my life after I was saved. They mentored me with encouragement, with words of wisdom and with understanding. They demonstrated the love of God to me. They took me with them into the heart of God as we spent many hours praying together. Thank you, Janie and Carolin, for the impact you had on my life as a new believer.

This book is also dedicated to my wonderful husband. We have been through many rough waters on the sea of matrimony. However, this book is not about those struggles, but rather, my personal journey as a Christian.

It stands without saying that the most important dedication of this book belongs to my Lord and Savior, Jesus Christ. Psalms 40:1-3 tells my story in an abbreviated form:

"*I waited patiently for the Lord; he turned to me and heard my cry. He lifted me out of the slimy pit, out of the mud and mire; he set my feet on a rock and gave me a firm place to stand. He put a new song in my mouth, a hymn of praise to our God. Many will see and fear and put their trust in the Lord.*"

ENDORSEMENTS

So many believers today are missing out on fully experiencing the Christian life because of effects of fear, rejection, shame, or generation sin patterns in their lives. In her book, our good friend, Judy Blanford, shares her personal testimony and teaching that will help set you free from the old nature and be an overcomer, participating in His divine nature. Judy is open and honest about the struggles she and her husband, Eldon, have overcome in their lives. Eldon and Judy's teachings have helped my wife and I and members of our congregation to be SET FREE! You can be too!

Pastors Barry and Kay Hill
Christian Life Church
Spokane, WA

I have been pastoring at Faith Family Church in Milton, WA since 1995. Shortly after arriving to fill the Youth Pastor position, my wife and I went through the Personal Freedom In Christ classes Judy and Eldon were teaching at the time. This book shares Judy's testimony and is consistent with what she and her husband have taught for over 20 years. In the book she is transparent and truthful. She did not try to hide anything and used her experiences in such a way that people will be able to connect with them. I know that the hearts of people will be touched and changed by reading this book. It contains keys to God's Kingdom and the abundant life we are intended to live. It is truth in action. **My Journey to the Throne** boldly and clearly teaches the Truth of God's Word and exhorts us to be the Church that reigns victorious over the gates of hell. (Matthew 16:13-19)

Pastor Greg Parsons
Faith Family Church
Milton, WA

We have known Eldon and Judy Blanford for many years and have received ministry and healing from the very principles that Judy talks about in this book. The principles that she discusses, if applied, will change your life. Great book with great life changing principles—a book that calls us to action. Judy's heart's desire is to see God's people receive freedom and to be able to reach the destiny that God has for each one of us. We recommend this book and support Blanford's ministry wholeheartedly.

Pastors Jerry and Gail Meyers

Freedom Center

Spanaway, WA

CONTENTS

ACKNOWLEDGEMENTS

After writing this book, I was introduced to Patricia Davenport. She agreed to take on the job of editor. Her credentials are many and impressive. It was an absolute blessing from God that she would consider helping an unknown, first-time author. I will be forever grateful for her expert guidance and the many hours she spent on this project. She is the editor, but more important to me, she is now my friend. Thank you, Patricia.

MY JOURNEY TO THE THRONE
(AND THINGS I HAVE LEARNED ALONG THE WAY)

By Judy Blanford

INTRODUCTION

"Daddy's Teenie Weenie" and "Mommy's Dolly." That is what I was called growing up. I was the third daughter in a family of four girls, was small for my age and rather scrawny so the names apparently fit me well. I was also shy, quiet, and timid, as well as being small. My oldest sister, who was usually able to get her own way about everything, was the dominant force in our family. The sister just older than I was self-confident and a little rebellious. My youngest sister was inquisitive and happy-go-lucky. She could get into and out of trouble very quickly.

We were raised in a Catholic home, trained in the Catholic religion, and held very closely to the church's teachings. We prayed the rosary every night during the Advent and Lenten seasons, attended Mass every Sunday and holy day, and went to special services for the Stations of the Cross, where we were reminded of the suffering Christ endured on our behalf. We didn't eat meat on Fridays, a rule that was abolished the first year after I was married in 1964. My mother took the three youngest children out of public school when I was in the fifth grade and drove us to a parochial school 21 miles away to ensure our protected Catholic upbringing.

I can never remember a time when I didn't believe in God. In fact, throughout most of my growing up years, I wanted to become a nun. I thought being a nun would bring me closer to God and perhaps ensure a place in purgatory where I could eventually be prayed into heaven.

We were raised by parents who loved us and did their very best to ensure that we had a solid moral groundwork laid in our lives. The things I will share in this book are not intended to cast a negative light on my parents or family or the church in which I was raised. They are simply my experiences as I lived my life before meeting Jesus, and the journey I have been on since my life-changing encounter with the living God. On the journey I have learned many lessons, and these pages you are holding contain some of the understanding I gleaned along the way. It is my hope that you will benefit from what you learn as much as I have. As I said earlier, as long as I can remember, I have always believed in God. However, I also had a tremendous fear of Him. In fact, I viewed Him as the "Great Scorekeeper in the Sky." This view was formed by the teachings in my early years about confession, penance and purgatory. In other words, I was taught that a person literally had to pay a price to get into heaven. As long as I believed this "lie" about God, I didn't want to get too close to Him. Drawing close to God would make my faults very obvious to Him and He would be angry with me.

It is my hope that by sharing with you my life experiences, the lies I believed and how I found God's Truth, the Holy Spirit will delve deeper into your own belief system. I pray that the "*God of our Lord Jesus Christ, the glorious Father, may give you the Spirit of wisdom and revelation, so that you may know him better. I pray also that the eyes of your heart may be enlightened in order that you may know the hope to which he has called you, the riches of his glorious inheritance in the saints...*" (Eph. 1:17-19a)

CHAPTER ONE

BAD GIRL

My conscience was always very active. This is a good thing, except when you can never shake the guilt and condemnation from your wrongdoings. Going to confession provided some temporary relief, but I knew that the priest didn't know how bad I really was, so how could he, or God, actually forgive me? I have come to know that an accusing, condemning conscience is fueled by Satan, the enemy of God. In Revelation 12:10 we are told that Satan stands before the throne of God constantly accusing the saints, *"…For the accuser of our brothers, who accuses them before our God day and night, has been hurled down."* Zechariah 3:1 tells us of the accusing ways of the enemy: *"Then he showed me Joshua the high priest standing before the angel of the Lord, and Satan standing at his right side to*

accuse him."

The Holy Spirit does not accuse or condemn. The Holy Spirit teaches and encourages us to walk on the path of truth and righteousness. Unfortunately, I didn't know about the Holy Spirit or His role in a believer's life as I was growing up. Consequently, I was always believing the lies that my conscience told me. *"But when He, the Spirit of Truth comes, He will guide you into all truth."* (John 16:13) The Holy Spirit has been faithful to perform this role in my life, and continues to do so daily. He has uncovered lies I believed and how I came to believe them—lies that kept me out of the throne room of God.

Ephesians 2:6-9 says, *"And God raised us up with Christ and seated us with Him in the heavenly realms in Christ Jesus, in order that in the coming ages He might show the incomparable riches of His grace, expressed in His kindness to us in Christ Jesus. For it is by grace you have been saved, through faith—and this not from yourselves, it is the gift of God."* The throne room is where we belong, seated next to the King of Kings and Lord of Lords. My feelings, belief system, fears and performance mentality brought me near the door, but never secure enough to enter in. The Holy Spirit showed me that God's Word is truth, not my feelings, belief system, fears or any other lie.

My first communion was a very significant spiritual event in my life. I was five years old, and what should have been a very holy moment, drawing me closer to God, became a source of guilt and shame. Let me explain.

The nuns teaching our Sunday School class made certain that we understood communion to be a very holy sacrament. We were taught that we were partaking of the actual body and blood of Jesus and that if we took communion with any sin in our heart, we would commit a mortal, or deadly, sin. If we died before confessing this mortal sin, we would go straight to hell.

In those days Catholics were not allowed to receive communion if they had eaten food or had drunk any liquids after midnight. My class was told that if you brushed your teeth before coming to Mass, and swallowed any of the toothpaste, you could not receive communion with the rest of the class because you had "eaten" something.

After brushing my teeth the morning of my first communion, I was afraid that I had, perhaps, swallowed some toothpaste, because the taste of it went down my throat. However, when asked if I had swallowed anything from midnight until we were lined up to walk down the church aisle, I told a half-truth and said "no." (After all, I wasn't absolutely certain I had swallowed any toothpaste.) I was even asked specifically, if I had swallowed any toothpaste. I was too afraid to admit to what my conscience was saying. I was already in line, I had my pretty white first communion dress on, as well as the special white shoes mom had bought for the event, and even a white veil. How could I sit through church with these clothes on and not participate with the other children receiving their first communion? Everyone would know that I was a bad girl if I wasn't with my class. And if I admitted that I had swallowed toothpaste, in order to be eligible for communion, I would have to go to confession first. In order to go to confession first, I would have to wait until the following Saturday and would miss receiving communion with the rest of my class that day.

What a dilemma for a five year old! Do I disappoint my mom and dad after they spent so much money on my new clothes? Do I risk looking bad in front of my classmates and the whole church? Do I have the integrity to admit my sin to my teachers? The answer to all those questions was "no," so I lied. Then the guilt really heaped upon me. I had committed three sins—I violated the church's rule about not eating before receiving communion, I lied when asked about it, and then I received communion with these mortal sins on my soul! I was bad. No doubt about it.

The enemy used this experience to reinforce guilt and confirm that I was no good. I just knew that I would always fall short of being acceptable to God. I believed Satan's lies and lived under the cloud of guilt, fear and condemnation. Other religious experiences added to the mantle of guilt and shame that I carried.

One Advent season my mother decided we needed to give Baby Jesus gifts of "good deeds" for His birthday. She put a crib scene in her bedroom. Every time we did a good deed, we could put half a toothpick in the empty crib. However, every time we were naughty or disrespectful, we had to take one of them out. I never saw myself as being good enough in anything I did. Therefore, all of my good deeds didn't really deserve to be a present for Jesus. No matter what or how much I did—that most people would consider good— my deeds didn't qualify as good. However, I would put some toothpicks in His crib anyway, because I didn't want the family to know I was a bad girl. For the same reason, I also didn't take toothpicks out when I was naughty. I was too ashamed, guilt-ridden, and fearful to admit my faults and risk ridicule or rejection. The present I gave Baby Jesus for

His birthday was a package of lies!

You can't really experience life the way God intends when you live in fear, rejection and shame. Jesus came to give us life and life more abundant. He wants us to live in the throne room with Him. The Apostle Paul must have had a deep understanding of God's love for him, if the prayers he prayed for the churches were from his personal experiences with God. Pray these prayers for yourself and see how the Holy Spirit begins to reveal God to you in deeper ways than you have known before: *"I pray also that the eyes of your heart may be enlightened in order that you may know the hope to which He has called you, the riches of His glorious inheritance in the saints, and his incomparably great power for us who believe."* (Ephesians 1:18-19a) *"I pray that out of His glorious riches He may strengthen you with power through His Spirit in your inner being, so that Christ may dwell in your hearts through faith. And I pray that you, being rooted and established in love, may have power, together with all the saints, to grasp how wide and long and high and deep is the love of Christ and to know this love that sur-passes knowledge—that you may be filled to the measure of all the fullness of God."* (Ephesians 3:16-19)

CHAPTER TWO

LIES WE BELIEVE

G od is a God of blessing. The amount of blessings God can bestow upon you will be limited if fear, rejection, shame, and regret are strongholds in your life. They will also erode the faith you do have so you will never be able to grasp, understand, and believe you are truly loved by God. You might believe that you cannot receive His love because you are too unworthy. Or if you do receive some blessings, they will be in a limited measure, because you can't expect God to work on your behalf more than once or twice.

I have struggled with the latter concept throughout my Christian life. I think the root of this belief system lies in something my mother told me after she acquiesced to my request for a favor. She said that she would allow it "this one time but don't expect me to allow it again." I think I transferred this concept to God—that He would do something for me once, but I couldn't expect Him to help me much after that. This belief system was reinforced by the old saying that I heard numerous times growing up, "God helps those who help themselves." If I hadn't done all I could do, it wasn't right to ask God for help. Of course, there was always more I could have done, because nothing I did was ever good enough. This led to the logical conclusion that I shouldn't be bothering God with my problems. I also remember being told that I shouldn't bother God about little things. He was busy enough solving problems of people more important than I. All these "lies" reinforced my beliefs about God and kept me at a distance from Him.

This concept, that I wasn't important enough to bother God, really runs counter to the Word of God which tells us that He only has His best in mind for us. *"For I know the plans I have for you, declares the Lord, plans to prosper you and not to harm you, plans to give you hope and a future."* (Jer. 29:11) Jesus said in Matthew 11:28, *"Come to me all you who are weary and burdened and I will give you rest."* First Peter 5:7 says, *"Cast all your anxiety on Him because He cares for you."* I could quote many other scriptures that prove my former belief system was wrong, but I think you get the point. Anything you believe that doesn't line up with the truth of God's Word needs to change. *"Do not conform any longer to the pattern of this world, but be transformed by the renewing of your mind. Then you will be able to test and approve what God's will is—his good, pleasing and perfect will."* (Romans 12:2)

CHAPTER THREE

TRUTH AS A LIFESTYLE

In Psalm 51:6 we are told, *"Surely you desire truth in the inner parts; you teach me wisdom in the inmost place."* God wants to work His Truth in the depth of our souls. There should be no room for deception to reside in the heart of a believer. *"Can both fresh water and salt water flow from the same spring?"* (James 3:11) However, it takes time to work God's Truth into our old nature.

God's Truth has not been worked as deep in my soul as it needs to be. For example, I still find myself thinking of excuses I could give a police officer if I were to be stopped for speeding. The excuses wouldn't be a real lie—after all, I am just going with the flow of the traffic. When confronted with something I did, or didn't do, I find

> **EXCUSE**
> **BLAME**
> **JUSTIFY**
> **DENY**

myself thinking of ways to defend myself, or at least make me look better than what a full admission of guilt would. The first thing Adam did after sinning was to cover himself with fig leaves and hide in the bushes. Instead of the glory of God covering Adam, he was covered with shame. He told God he was hiding because of "this woman" God gave him. The fallen nature responds with excusing, blaming, justifying and denying—beating around the bush. Anytime you find yourself **excusing, blaming, justifying or denying,** there is a good chance you are not walking in God's Truth!

God is the Father of Truth. Satan is the father of lies. If we are born again children of God, we should reflect His character and nature. Therefore, we should all be children of Truth. Please understand that to walk in Truth doesn't give us license to hurt others with our opinions. Speaking the truth in love is very different from speaking our opinions in judgment.

Unfortunately, we are all born with sinful natures as a result of the Fall of man. Paul said in Romans 7:25b, "… *So then, I myself in my mind am a slave to God's law, but in the sinful nature a slave to the law of sin.*" When we are born again our spirit is new. In John 3: 5 he states, "*Jesus answered, I tell you the truth, no one can enter the kingdom of God unless he is born of water and the Spirit. Flesh gives birth to flesh, but the Spirit gives birth to spirit.*" After our spirit is born again or saved, Philippians 2:12 tells us to "... *work out your salvation.*" Your salvation is in your spirit. Now it needs to be worked into your soul realm—your mind, will and emotions. This is accomplished by:

- <u>Renewing your mind</u>: "*Do not conform any longer to the pattern of this world, but be transformed by the renewing of your mind.*" (Rom. 12:2) Your mind is renewed by reading and applying the Word of God to your life.

- <u>The submission of your will to God:</u> "*...yet not my will, but yours be done.*" (Luke 22:42) Sometimes we can be so accustomed to thinking we are always right, or having things our way, that it is difficult to even consider seeking God's way of doing things let alone submitting to it. "*For my thoughts are not your thoughts, neither are your ways my ways, declares the Lord. As the heavens are higher than the earth, so are my ways higher than your ways and my thoughts than your thoughts.*" (Isaiah 55:8-9) Perhaps you have been told, "God gave you a brain. Use it!" Submitting to God doesn't mean we don't use the brain He gave us.

It means that we submit our thoughts to Him to know what He is thinking about the problem.

• <u>Receiving the healing He has for your emotions</u>: "*He was despised and rejected by men, a man of sorrows, and familiar with suffering. Like one from whom men hide their faces he was despised, and we esteemed him not. Surely he took up our infirmities and carried our sorrows, yet we considered him stricken by God, smitten by him, and afflicted. But he was pierced for our transgressions, he was crushed for our iniquities; the punishment that brought us peace was upon him, and by his wounds we are healed.*" (Isaiah 53:3-5) Christ took all our rejection, sorrows, suffering, afflictions, infirmities, sins and our very iniquitous nature upon the cross. In exchange, He gave us forgiveness, healing and peace. We must be willing to forgive others just as Christ forgives us in order to appropriate His healing power.

I want to share with you now more of my personal testimonies to let you know it is possible to come out of the old nature and participate in His divine nature: "*His divine power has given us everything we need for life and godliness* *through our knowledge of him who called us by his own glory and goodness. Through these he has given us his very great and precious promises, so that through them **you may participate in the divine nature** and escape the corruption in the world caused by evil desires."* (2 Pet. 1:3-4)

Chapter Four

ROOTS OF REJECTION

As stated earlier, I was the third daughter in a family of four girls. My parents wanted a son to carry on the Jefferson name. My father was the only boy in his family and thus, the only child through whom this noble name could be passed.

God began the soul-healing process in my life at age 42. Until then, I always felt that I was on the outside looking in. I thought maybe I was adopted. I felt I could never measure up and always fell short of pleasing my mother. My other sisters didn't seem to struggle with these feelings, although, honestly, I never really had the courage to talk with them about how I felt. I think I was afraid they would confirm that there was something wrong with me, so I never talked about my fears with them.

I was saved when I was 35. God revealed Himself to me as the "God of Love!" I was at a Catholic weekend retreat. I had gone to confession and told the priest my sins, one of which was bitterness towards my parish priest. He gave me absolution and then assigned my penance. I went into the chapel to be alone to pray the prayers that would absolve me of my guilt. All of a sudden Jesus was sitting beside me, loving me, and taking joy in being with me! He absolved me from my guilt and He forgave my sins before I said my penance. He washed over me with His love. The room seemed to light up with His presence. I stayed with Him in the chapel for over an hour.

I didn't want to leave, but I was already late to the next meeting. The rules of the weekend required attendance at every meeting, so I reluctantly got up and left the chapel. On the way to the meeting room, I ducked into a prayer room and fell on my knees with arms outstretched, praising this awesome, loving God I had just met personally.

I knew I was loved and God wasn't waiting up in heaven to catch me doing wrong so He could condemn me. WOW! What a radical shift in my belief system! When I finally walked into the classroom (about an hour and a half late) I was apparently "glowing" with the presence of God.

Someone commented later that she could see Jesus come in the room with me.

I have never been the same. However, I wasn't instantly healed of the soul wounds I had carried over the past years. The difference was simply that I knew in my heart that God and Jesus loved me. My mind and emotions still held on to the old nature with its sin patterns and hurts. **Salvation isn't the end of our journey, it is only the beginning.**

From my salvation experience until now, I have had a burning passion for the Word of God. *"Do not be conformed any longer to the pattern of this world, but be transformed by the renewing of your mind."* (Rom. 12:2) The Word of God began to renew my mind and open my heart to the healing power of Jesus Christ in every area of my life.

I knew that I needed a lot of emotional healing, but at that point I didn't know how to get it. When I had been a Christian about eight years, I read the book, "You Can Be Emotionally Free," by Rita Bennett. It was filled with scriptural references to emotional healing, and testimonies of people who had received emotional healing. This gave me hope that the immature, childish person inside of me could "grow up." However, I didn't know Rita Bennett or any of the people she had trained to minister inner healing, so I assumed I would never benefit from her knowledge. God had other ideas. Jesus sent the Holy Spirit to be my Counselor. *"And I will ask the Father, and he will give you another Counselor to be with you forever—the Spirit of Truth."* (John 14:16-17a) The following was the first emotional healing that I experienced:

I was alone one evening, which was a rare occurrence. We had four teenagers in our home at the time—our three children and a nephew. I was enjoying the quiet house and spending time with the Lord. I wasn't seeking anything from Him, but out of nowhere, He spoke to my heart and told me He wanted to heal my emotions. I knew I was a mess so I told Him it was about time.

What I mean by saying I was a mess is that I had a very immature response system within me. I was easily offended. I responded to negative circumstances, situations, and people by withdrawing and avoiding others, including my husband and children. I shut down emotionally and hardened my heart so I wouldn't be vulnerable the next time they hurt me. I knew these responses were childish, but it seemed hopeless for me to change. I had always been this way.

In I Corinthians 13:11 Paul says, *"When I was a child, I talked like a child, I thought like a child, reasoned like a child. When I became a man, I put childish ways behind me.*" I was still responding in immature, childish ways. I was like a 42 year old woman with an eight or ten year old girl trapped inside of me. I felt like such a phony. I didn't feel like a woman emotionally, as much as I felt like a child.

Emotional healing is based on the scriptures that tell us God is omnipresent—or everywhere all the time:

- Psalm 139:7-12: "*Where can I go from your Spirit? Where can I flee from your presence? If I go up to the heavens, you are there; if I make my bed in the depths, you are there. If I rise on the wings of the dawn, if I settle on the far side of the sea, even there your hand will guide me, your right hand will hold me fast. If I say, 'Surely the darkness will hide me and the light become night around me.' Even the darkness will not be dark to you; the light will shine like the day, for darkness is as light to you.*"

- Jeremiah 23:23-24: "*Am I only a God nearby, declares the Lord, and not a God far away? Can anyone hide in secret places so that I cannot see him? Declares the Lord. Do not I fill the heaven and earth? Declares the Lord.*"

- Acts 17:27-28: "*God did this so that men would seek him and perhaps reach out for him and find him, though he is not far from each one of us. For in him we live and move and have our being."*

There has never been a time that God has been unaware of you. He actually *"created your inmost being; (He) knit you together in your mother's womb."* (Psalm 139:13) Maybe your parents didn't want you, or wanted a son instead of a daughter or vice versa. However, God wanted you! He chose you in Christ *"before the creation of the world to be holy and blameless in His sight."* (Ephesians 1:4)

This knowledge actually makes some people mad at God. "If God is such a loving and all-knowing God, why did He let such terrible things happen to me as a child?" We have to balance the goodness and love of God with the fact that he gave man a free will. It was never God's will that bad things happen to His creation; however, it is Satan's will to influence mankind to follow him instead of God. It is man's choice whom he will follow. That is why Jesus had to become a man and become sin for us. He redeemed us from the effects of our fallen nature and thus provided a way for us to take on the divine nature as 2 Peter 1:3-4 tells us.

Jesus actually took all of our sin, our iniquitous nature, our emotional wounds and physical diseases on the cross when He died. He arose with none of the negative things clinging to Him. If we can truly die to self, He can help us become alive in Him. Paul says in Galatians 2:20, "*I have been crucified with Christ and I no longer live, but Christ lives in me. For the life I live in the body, I live by faith in the Son of God, who loved me and gave himself for me.*"

He loves you and me. He gave Himself for us so we could live a life that will bring glory to His Name. How many Christians have you met, and maybe you are one, who are always under their circumstances? They profess Christ as Savior, but live far below the poverty line when it comes to abundant life. By poverty line, I don't mean financial as much as emotional and physical.

I lived below the poverty line for 42 years. The night Jesus said He wanted to heal my emotions was a turning point in my Christian and adult life. Here's what happened.

I submitted myself to whatever God wanted to do, not sure what it would be. He took me back to the time when I was born. It was as if the adult Judy was in the delivery room watching the baby Judy being born. When the doctor announced to my mother that she had another baby girl, the Lord showed me that her response was, "Oh no. Not another girl!" I don't know if she actually said those words, but by not producing a son, she felt like she had failed my father. With her response, a spirit of rejection had access to my soul. My mother had no idea of the spiritual ramifications that her response regarding my gender had, but Satan takes advantage of any opportunity he has to steal, kill and destroy.

With this spiritual experience I gained understanding as to why I always felt like I was on the outside looking in, or that there was something wrong with me. Everything that I experienced was filtered through that spirit of rejection. I perceived rejection if a friend was preoccupied with something and didn't notice me when I walked in a room. I immediately thought she was mad at me and wondered what I had done wrong. Then I would reject her before she could reject me!

The dynamics of rejection and fear of rejection are insidious. Rejection and fear of rejection become a snowball that will wrap you up and keep you "ice"-olated emotionally and physically from people. At least, that is how it worked in my life, and in our 25 years of ministry experience, my husband and I have seen it work the same way in the lives of many others.

I gained great understanding from what the Lord showed me in the vision of the delivery room. However, understanding doesn't heal the soul. Jesus does. The delivery room vision continued.

I was letting the understanding of the rejection issues in my life sink in, when Jesus hit the replay button on this spiritual video of my birth. This time He was there. He is omnipresent, so He was in that delivery room with me. As the doctor announced my gender to my mom, I looked over and saw Jesus. He had tears of joy streaming down His face. He held this little baby girl up as if proudly showing me to His Father, and said, "Father, look. We have another baby girl for our kingdom!" I didn't even hear my mother's response. I heard Jesus say that I was exactly what He created me to be—a girl! And I felt His joy. He chose me from the foundation of the world. I was fulfilling His plan. It was okay to be a girl!

You see, I could never really please my mother because I couldn't change my gender. As long as she looked at me through the eyes of her failure and disappointment, that is what I became to her. She did not intentionally reject me. She loved me as much as disappointment would allow. Even the name she chose for me reflected her sense of failure. Mom's first choice for my name was Jude. However, in the Catholic Church girl babies could not be named after male saints. St.

Jude was a man, so she named me Judith which was as close as she could come to Jude without violating Catholic law or tradition. St. Jude was the Patron Saint of Hopeless Causes. Even my name reflected the hopelessness my gender caused her. Satan takes advantage of every opportunity to bring rejection into our lives. This was a prime opportunity and rejection became a part of my life.

With the knowledge that I pleased my Lord and Savior, I was able to forgive my mother for her unintentional sin. The filter of rejection was removed from me when I forgave. I actually felt ten pounds lighter. That filter no longer functioned. I could begin to respond to people and life circumstances through reality, not rejection.

What a difference! I began to grow up spiritually and emotionally. My husband and children noticed a difference in my countenance. The journey to emotional maturity started. Now I had hope that I could actually put the childish ways behind me.

Chapter Five

FEAR OF REJECTION
AND FEAR OF ABANDONMENT

The next major emotional healing the Lord provided for me exposed the elusive power of two fears—the fear of rejection and fear of abandonment. These fears are common to man. However, I thought that because I was delivered from rejection and abandonment, that I was all done with those demonic influences. This next testimony is how the Lord revealed these fears, delivered me from them, and healed my soul.

Eldon and I had been married over 25 years and we had never really raised our voices to each other in anger. We had gotten angry many times, but instead of dealing with the anger, we shut each other out emotionally. The iceberg between us grew. I didn't trust him with my emotional needs, so I seldom shared my heart with him, nor did he share his heart issues with me.

Now mind you, we looked as if we had it all together. We were leaders in our church, taught Sunday School together, were state directors of a growing marriage ministry, and Eldon was president of the local Full Gospel Business Men's Fellowship International. We had three children in private Christian colleges and he was a successful businessman. But in Matthew 23:27-28 Jesus said, *"Woe to you, teachers of the law and Pharisees, you hypocrites! You are like white-washed tombs, which look beautiful on the outside but on the inside are full of dead men's bones and everything unclean. In the same way, on the outside you appear as righteous but on the inside you are full of hypocrisy and wickedness."* It all looked good from the outside (whitewashed tombs) but our marriage was full of dead men's bones. I wonder how many couples are like that in the church today—living below the poverty line in their Father's house. We enter into His abundant life when we let Him heal our heart, not just put on our church face for a Sunday morning show, like the Pharisees did. Jesus called the Pharisees hypocrites.

If you know there are issues in your heart and that you are basically living a pharisaical life, admit this to God. Don't let your pride keep you from the healing He wants to do in you. You will have more joy and peace than you ever had, and you will be a vessel fit for the King. One of my all-time favorite scriptures is in II Timothy 2:20-21, *"In a large house there are articles not only of gold and silver, but also of wood and clay; some are for noble purposes and some for ignoble. If a man cleanses himself from the latter, he will be an instrument for noble purposes, made holy, useful to the Master and prepared to do any good work."*

When I looked up the word, ignoble, it basically means something that was used for garbage or human waste. Over the years my husband and I have ministered to many people who have been physically and verbally abused. Some have been called words that mean human waste, and have even had excrement smeared on them by a parent. They have been made to feel like a curse to parents, grandparents, siblings and others. They feel like they are a mistake. Instead of having real worth or value to anyone, they were made to feel that they were of negative value and a bother to have around. But the above scripture says that we can be *"cleansed from the ignoble purposes and become instruments for noble purposes, made holy, useful to the Master and prepared to do any good work."*

The healings and deliverances I am sharing with you are

the ways God cleansed me from the ignoble purposes the enemy had for my life. As I shared earlier, my very name, Judith, reflected the hopelessness my mother had in ever producing that son to carry on the Jefferson family name. The Holy Spirit showed me I had to forgive my mom.

My husband and I broke the power of the curse of hopelessness over my life by taking authority over the curse, and laying it at the cross. Jesus became a curse for me (Galatians 3:13). I no longer have to carry that curse. We then released me into the blessing of my name, thus reversing the curse. Now I have become a vessel of hope to others. *What the enemy intended for harm, God intended for good!* (Gen. 50:20)

Through Jesus Christ, God has provided healing for every wound and victory over every curse or demonic power that comes against His children. We just have to appropriate the work of the cross and get cleansed from the ignoble powers at work in our lives. The following is an example of how the Holy Spirit revealed the hidden strongholds of fear of rejection and fear of abandonment in my life, and how we appropriated the work of the cross to gain victory over them.

The fear of rejection and fear of abandonment still lurked in the recesses of my soul. The circumstances God used to reveal them were difficult to negotiate, particularly since my husband and I never really dealt with the hurts and anger we had toward one another. We did as our parents had done— we shoved our problems under the rug and hoped they would go away.

One day my husband and I had a fight and we actually spoke angry words to each other. However, after the words came out, we went back into our old pattern and never addressed the anger, causes for the anger, the words that were spoken, or our feelings. The iceberg grew wider and thicker than ever before. The only thing that I was encouraged about in the whole situation was that we actually did express our anger. Previously, we couldn't risk expressing our anger for fear of rejection.

The Word tells us in Ephesians 4:26, "*In your anger do not sin: Do not let the sun go down while you are angry.*" I began to pray that God would help us to deal with our anger in a Scriptural way. We sinned in our anger by holding unforgiveness and judgments against each other. We sinned by letting the sun go down on our anger for three days! Lord, help us to be angry and sin not. We got through that episode but another was on its way.

Six months later, another incident came up. I questioned

Eldon regarding a revelation he said God gave him. I asked how he would line this revelation up with a couple of different scriptures. He became very angry because he thought I always had to be right and that I never trusted anything he said. He stormed out of the house. Again, it was three days before we talked to each other. This situation led to a healing Eldon received in his soul. Let me share it with you also, because it caused a significant shift in our relationship. Men can need healing in their souls as much as women do.

When Eldon was in the first grade, their class visited a local historical site where the town's founder signed his name on a rock by the river. His signature ratified a treaty with the Native Americans in the area. On the way home from school that day, Eldon and two of his friends decided to revisit that site. Afterwards, Eldon turned and walked down the railroad tracks toward his home. He was forty-five minutes late getting home and he knew his mother would not be happy. The other two boys wanted to stay and play at the river.

At 7:30 p.m. that night, there was a knock on the door. It was the local police chief. He wanted to talk with Eldon. Eldon was scared. He was already in trouble with his mother for coming home late from school. What on earth did the policeman want from him? He was questioned about the whereabouts of his two friends. The policeman didn't want to accept Eldon's answer that he left them at the river and came home and he hadn't seen them since. Eldon was perplexed as to why the officer wouldn't believe him. When he asked his mother about it, she told him that if he had come home when he was supposed to, no one would be asking him questions.

The next day at school, the principal and other law enforcement officials joined in the questioning process. It was at this point that Eldon found out that one of the two boys had fallen into the river and drowned. The other boy was so traumatized that he couldn't talk. Eldon was one of the last two people to see this unfortunate classmate alive, and was the only person from whom the authorities could get information. He couldn't understand why they wouldn't believe him and why they kept questioning him.

From that day on, whenever Eldon was challenged to defend his position or was even asked for an explanation, he would get defensive. This led to a lot of unresolved issues in our relationship, and in other relationships. If I asked a question for clarity purposes, or to help me understand his thinking process, he would immediately get defensive in his response. I was afraid of his anger, so I would usually drop the matter.

We were in the third day of our latest cold war, when we decided to pray about our issue. While we were praying, the Lord brought back to Eldon the memory of his class-mate who drowned, and he shared that memory with me. We knew it must have some significance, but did not know what it could be. We also knew the importance of forgiving, so he went through the process of forgiving everyone in that trau-matic memory. After forgiving, the memory was replayed in Eldon's mind. In the replay, Jesus was present with him and He called for Eldon to come home. They walked together down the railroad tracks. Part way home, Eldon asked Jesus, "But why didn't you call my two friends to come home, too?" Jesus answered him, "I did, but they didn't listen."

The memory went immediately to the living room of Eldon's home. The police officer knocked on the front door. When the door was opened, Jesus was with Eldon. He had his arm around Eldon's shoulder, protecting the little boy and showing belief and trust in him. Eldon no longer had to defend himself. He had a defender. The little boy's soul was healed.

The Holy Spirit revealed the defensive response pat-tern that had been cemented in him the day of that tragic incident. Eldon gave the Holy Spirit permission to change this response pattern and asked His help to do so. He also asked the Holy Spirit to help him become more like Jesus, patient and loving instead of angry and defensive. He began to change that night.

The healing Eldon experienced paved the way for my healing and deliverance from the fear of rejection and fear of abandonment, when the third episode of anger happened six months later.

God blessed us with a business that required a limited amount of time to serve our clients. Eldon did not like to be asked to do anything else when he was busy with his work. One day he and I were both in the bedroom about 1 p.m. in the afternoon. Since he seemed to be in a good mood, and was only a few feet away from the furnace, I asked him if he would change the furnace filter while he was so close. He exploded in angry indignation, accusing me of always asking him to do things on his "busy days." He stomped into the laundry room where the furnace is located, noisily took the old filter out, replaced it with a new filter I had placed next to the furnace and stormed out to the garbage can with the old filter. I stood where I was, in a stunned and para-lyzed state, as I listened to him bang around and slam the galvanized metal garbage can lid down.

All of a sudden anger and fury rose up within me. I realized I had done nothing wrong in asking him to take care of this household chore, and I did not deserve to be blamed for his anger. I was not responsible for his reaction! I went storming into the kitchen next to his office and proceeded to rant and rave so loud I was concerned about the neighbors hearing our furious exchange. Eldon was yelling back at me and told me to go out to the garbage can and look at the filter, because it wasn't even dirty. I gave him a salute and shouted, "YES, SIR!" several times, and went outside. When I saw the filter, it appeared to be relatively clean. Oh no! I had asked him to do an unnecessary chore and interrupted his day. I went back into the house and saluted him again. I told him, "YOU WERE RIGHT, SIR!! I WILL NEVER ASK YOU TO DO ANOTHER THING IN MY LIFE, SIR!!"

I can never remember being so angry, hurt, demeaned and confused. I left the house and went to the Christian book store. I was hyperventilating so bad that I thought I might pass out. However, after arriving, I realized that if I passed out and an ambulance was called, this would be an even greater disruption to his precious time. He would be even more angry with me. I went home.

After walking through his office and trying to completely ignore him, he stopped me in the kitchen and asked me to forgive him. The Lord had been dealing with him about the pain he caused me with his words, attitudes and actions. Eldon had even asked the Lord to let him feel the pain I felt—and God did. It was out of that pain that he asked my forgiveness. However, there was nothing inside me that wanted to forgive him. I knew what the Word of God says about the importance of forgiving, but there was no way I ever wanted to talk to him again, or forgive him for anything!

I went into our bedroom and locked both doors. I got on my knees beside the bed and cried out to the Lord. I told Him that I had been asking Him to show us how to be angry and not sin, but things were getting worse instead of better. I begged Him to help me, to show me what to do, and I wasn't getting any answers.

Then there was a knock on the bedroom door. Eldon asked if he could come in. I didn't want to let him in, but I had been asking God to help me allow my husband into the inner recesses of my heart. I had many reasons why it was difficult to do this, not the least of which was the infidelity in past years. Jesus had been my Comforter, Companion, and Healer. He took good care of my heart. I didn't need or trust

Eldon with my heart. But the Holy Spirit let me know He was answering my prayers, so I needed to unlock my bedroom door—and my heart also.

I got up and opened the door, then went back to the bedside where I knelt in tears. Eldon put his arm around me as I cried. He again asked me to forgive him. A memory came to my mind. The memory was of a time when my dad got angry. My mother's reaction to my dad's anger was to avoid him, to get out of his way, to walk on eggshells—whatever she had to do until the anger subsided. She told all four of us girls to get out of dad's way.

I ran down the basement stairs and hid my face in the recreation room couch. Dad slammed the back door at the top of the stair landing so hard that it broke the door's window pane. Dad was never physically abusive to any of us, but he did have a temper. To me, when Dad got mad, he became ten feet tall. I reacted to his anger the way my mother did, because that was what I was taught.

I did not want to share this memory with Eldon, but knew I had to. As I began to share, I found myself talking like a little girl. "Daddy, don't go!" "Daddy, I'll be good!" "Daddy, don't go!" I had taken false responsibility for my father's anger. I had taken false responsibility for Eldon's anger. That false responsibility got too heavy to carry and that is why I exploded in anger myself.

Eldon discerned from this memory and my "little girl" response to my father's anger, that the fear of rejection and the fear of abandonment were demonic forces fueling this anger. He took authority over them and ordered them to leave. I physically felt a release in my soul and body.

I was able to forgive Eldon. I also had to ask him to forgive me for shutting him out and give him permission to enter the inner sanctuary of my heart. We prayed for each other, then he left and resumed his work.

I crawled up on the bed and asked the Lord to bring good out of this whole mess. Romans 8:28 says, "*...in all things God works for the good of those who love him, who have been called according to his purpose.*" And Paul said in Philippians 1:19b,"*...and the help given by the Spirit of Jesus Christ, what has happened to me will turn out for my deliverance.*" The Lord showed me His presence in the midst of that memory.

After dad left the house, Jesus called to me from the landing where the glass was shattered. I went to the bottom of the stairs but would not come up to Jesus. He picked up a shard of glass and held it in the empty space where the window had been. He said, "Look." As I looked, strong, clear glass began to fill the empty place. He said, "I can make you stronger and more beautiful than you have ever been." With His presence and His assurance that He was working everything together for our good and my deliverance, my soul received healing. I fell into a peaceful sleep.

The deliverance from the fear of rejection and fear of abandonment has brought much peace to my soul. In the course of praying for each other, we recognized that because of my fearful reaction to a man's anger, Eldon began to use my fear to avoid dealing with uncomfortable issues. If he even looked as if he were getting angry, I would back off and even apologize for something I didn't do, if that was necessary to avoid his anger. He is no dummy. He learned fairly quickly to use anger to his advantage. When you couple this with his already defensive reactions when questioned, an atmosphere was created in our relationship that did not allow conflicts to be resolved or healed.

From that day until now, we have not had another explosive exchange of anger. That is not to say we have not been angry with one another. It simply means that the Lord has truly set us free to be angry and not sin. We are more apt to listen to each other without judging. We can more quickly repent of our own pride and self-righteousness that fuels conflicts. And we can more quickly confess our sins to one another and pray for each other that we might be healed from each other's sins. (James 5:16) We are not perfect in responding this way, but are continuing to improve.

CHAPTER SIX

SINS THAT FUEL STRIFE

If I may, I would like to use this life example of strife in the preceding chapter to teach some very important scriptural understanding we have learned. It has to do with the source of conflict. James 3:16 (NIV) says, *"For where you have envy and selfish ambition, there you find disorder and every evil practice."* The King James version says: *"For where envying and strife is, there is confusion and every evil work."* Selfish ambition and strife are synonymous terms. Selfish ambition is basically where each person wants his or her own way, regardless of what the other's thoughts, feelings or facts are in a matter. It could also be that you have to be right and therefore, the other person has to be wrong. You won't accept anything short of being on the top—being the winner, no matter what.

Selfish ambition causes strife and contention in relationships. A contributing sin behind strife is found in Proverbs 22:10, *"Drive out the mocker and out goes strife; quarrels and insults are ended."*

When the Lord highlighted that scripture to me, I was rather confused because I didn't see myself as a mocker. I always thought of a mocker as someone who spit on Jesus. I had never even thought of doing that, therefore, I couldn't be a mocker. The Lord was patient with my protests of innocence. Then He asked me, "How do you respond when your husband gives you correction?"

I thought about it, but didn't want to admit what was really in my heart. My first response to my husband's correction would have been thoughts such as, "What makes you think YOU are right and I am wrong? Why do YOU always have to be right and I have to be wrong?" The Lord said, "That is a mocking spirit." Oh my! I had been trying to drive it out of my husband for years and it was in me also!

You cannot use the enemy's tools to bring about Godly changes. It only drives the person you are working on further from you and from God. Besides, none of us was ever given the job of being the Holy Spirit for others. The only heart we are able to change with the Holy Spirit's help is our own. Then, as our own heart is cleansed and made holy, we will reflect God's love to others. Love will draw more people to Jesus than all the words we speak. In fact, if we don't have love, our words will only be clanging cymbals and resounding gongs. (I Cor. 13:1) People get tired of that noise, but words spoken in love find their way into hungry, hurting hearts and produce a good crop.

Another scripture that reveals contributing sin behind strife and mockery is found in Proverbs 21:24, *"The proud and arrogant man— 'Mocker' is his name; he behaves with overweening pride."*

Behind strife is a mocking spirit. Behind a mocking spirit is pride and arrogance. When you are dealing with strife in a relationship, you will always have to address the strongman of pride in your own heart. Pride is at the base of our fallen nature. Satan fell from heaven because of his pride.

The basic definition of pride boils down to a concern with self over a concern for others. I want my way. My way is right. My way is best. I need this more than you do. I am justified when I break the law because I have special circum-stances that should circumvent the law. Whatever excuse you use, "I" is usually in the middle of it. "I" translates to pride whenever strife is present. "I" is the middle letter of sin.

I have learned that the best way to handle strife is to get alone and ask the Lord to show me my heart. My husband does the same thing. The Lord will be faithful to reveal those things hidden in our hearts. That is His job. Psalm 139:23-24 says, *"Search me, O God, and know my heart; test me and know my anxious thoughts. See if there is any offensive way in me, and lead me in the way everlasting."* (Psalm 139:23-24) *"The lamp of the Lord searches the spirit of a man; it searches out his inmost being."* (Proverbs 20:27) When we give God permission to do His work, we may not always like what He shows us, but He will do what we give Him permission to do.

After seeing and confessing our sins we are cleansed from all the unrighteousness that these sins bring. This is the application of I John 1:9, *"If we confess our sins, he is faithful and just and will forgive us our sins and purify us from all unrighteousness."* Now we are a clean vessel.

However, the heart of the one with whom we had strife may still be wounded. It is then important to confess your sin(s) to the one with whom you had the strife and ask his or her forgiveness. Follow this by praying for his or her heart to be healed. James 5:16 says, *"Therefore confess your sins to each other and pray for each other so that you may* be healed. *The prayer of a righteous man is powerful and effective.*"

Strife can leave fear in others, especially when it results in name-calling and/or physical intimidation or violence. These wounds need healing. A righteous man (woman) will recognize and repent of the sins God shows him or her, and follow the pattern scripture gives us to bring about healing. A righteous man's prayers are powerful and effective. An unrighteous man's prayers that include **excusing, blaming, justifying,** and **denying** will result in more hurt.

Example: "Oh God, I see that I hurt my spouse with the filthy, demeaning words I spoke. But God, if you hadn't given me this self-righteous person for a mate, I would never have spoken so harshly. If he/she would only learn to keep his/her mouth shut I wouldn't be this way. But honey, please forgive me and I pray that God will heal your heart." This example could be expanded upon but I think you get the picture.

Whenever you find yourself **excusing, blaming, justifying** or **denying**, you are not taking ownership of the sin in your heart. I John 1:9 says if we confess our sin He will forgive us and cleanse us. It doesn't say if we confess our spouse's or other's sins, then our sin will be forgiven. **In fact,**

if you confess with excuses, blaming others for your sin, justifying or denying, you have essentially covered your sin with your own rationale. The blood of Jesus does not work because you have justified yourself. Adam started this in the garden after he and Eve sinned. Genesis 3:12 says, *"The man said, 'The woman you put here with me—she gave me some fruit from the tree, and I ate it.'"* This is a very human response, but it comes out of the fallen nature—not the nature of God. This was Adam's response after he sinned. We are to participate in God's divine nature to *"escape the corruption in the world caused by evil desires."* (II Pet. 1:4) His divine nature is the nature Adam and Eve had before they sinned. God's divine nature does not bring guilt, blame and shame on others. Quite the contrary—His divine nature cleanses us from guilt, blame and shame.

We were ministering to a couple many years ago. Their marriage would fall into a ditch about every six months and we would put a band aid of prayer on them and send them home. We had concerns about the sin we were seeing in both of them, but hesitated to tell them what we saw. We were afraid to hurt their feelings or give the impression that we thought we were "holier" than they were. After all, he was an assistant youth pastor in a local church. Who were we to tell them they were sinners?

One day she made an emergency call to us after he had thrown an ax at her. As they were sitting on our couch the next day, he explained why he was so angry that he threw the ax. His explanation included the **excusing, blaming, justifying and denying** that all of us do. He said she wasn't a compassionate enough wife. He tried to justify and excuse himself, and denied that he had done anything wrong. After all, he said, he didn't hit her with the ax. I couldn't believe what I was hearing, and began silently asking the Lord how we should handle this situation. I shall never forget what the Holy Spirit told me, "You stop beating

Call sin what it is— SIN

around the bush with these people. You start calling sin, SIN!"

From that time forward we have tried to identify the sin that is causing problems in a relationship. Adam and Eve never had any problems in the garden until they sinned. Every problem people experience in relationships will have its base in sin. We have already covered how pride is the chief culprit. Pride, anger, unforgiveness and many other sins were included in the incident mentioned above. As this couple repented of their sins and forgave one another, we prayed for their hearts to be healed from the effects of their sins. We then took authority over the strongholds of pride and anger.

Later, the Lord showed us the scriptural basis for ministering in this way. It is found in Lamentations 2:14, *"The visions of your prophets were false and worthless; they did not expose your sin to ward off your captivity. The oracles they gave you were false and misleading."* If we do not expose the sin of those to whom we minister, we will be a false prophet and they will be held captive to their sins. The couple cited above was made aware of their sins of pride, unforgiveness, judgments, revenge, anger, etc. They had no idea they were sinning in these ways. They were so used to **excusing, blaming, justifying and denying**, that it never occurred to them that they each had sin in their own heart. They would have remained captive to their sins had they not been exposed. Praise the Lord they had teachable spirits and responded in humility, repentance and forgiveness. Several years later they moved and started a church. They were cleansed from the ignoble purposes (sin) from which the enemy had kept them ignorant and they became vessels fit for the King.

CHAPTER SEVEN

GENERATIONAL SIN

In my Christian journey I have also had to deal with generational sins. Generational sins are basically patterns of sin that are passed on to us because they are in the family line. For instance, have you ever heard statements such as, "All the Jones boys are angry men. Their fathers and grandfathers were angry, too." If you are one of the Jones boys or girls, you might think that there is no escape from this destiny. Generational sin can influence or even determine our identity, and thus, our destiny, but it doesn't have to control us. As born-again children of God, we no longer have to conform to the pattern of this world. We are new creations, and we don't have to live as we have in the past, or as other family members live.

Jesus said, "*...by their fruit you will recognize them.*"

(Mt. 7:20) What is the fruit on your family tree? You can hide behind these generational patterns and use them as an excuse not to change, but if you are a born-again member of God's family, He wants you to take on His character and nature. In order to set your course in this direction, there are scriptural steps you must take when you recognize a generational sin:

- admit to God that it is your sin,
- forgive your parents for the inheritance of this sin,
- ask God to forgive you,
- then renounce this sinful nature.

This is when God can begin to transform you by the renewing of your mind, bringing forth the mind of Christ within you. Then you can discover and embrace your true identity.

PERSONAL EXAMPLES

Self-Pity

I had a lot of self-pity in my life. The Lord began to show me that it was generational, coming from my father's side of the family. I can remember my father frequently expecting to be last or left out. I took this even further by comparing the gifts I received at Christmas and other occasions, with what my sisters received. Of course, mine were never as good as theirs. This self-pity slopped over into God's gifts and love—I was never as blessed as others, or so I thought.

Self-pity usually has several partners that come along for the ride. In my case they were envy, jealousy and competition. Even after becoming a Christian, I would look at how God was blessing others, compare their works with mine, feel self-pity because I was doing more and getting less, and end up being envious and jealous. It was a deep pit that led to anger, bitterness, depression and distance from God.

Unforgiveness

There is also the sin of unforgiveness on my father's side of the family. In doing genealogical research on our family, one of my sisters uncovered letters giving evidence to three generations of family members who died with unforgiveness in their hearts. My father struggled with this, and my oldest sister is consumed by it. She has passed it on to her children. Without spiritual awakening in Christ and repentance, her grandchildren will be contaminated by it also.

Generational Sin

My sister has uncovered evidence of generational sexual sin. She found out that my grandmother on mom's side was an illegitimate child. We don't know about mom's generation, but my generation had sexual sin as well. The fruit on Eldon's family tree was riddled with sexual immorality and deception.

My mother's mother had a critical spirit. My mother was very critical also and I have struggled with that generational sin—seeing the negative instead of the positive.

It is true that most people struggle with the same or similar sins. However, if you can identify most of your family members as being, for example, angry, sexually immoral, deceptive, critical and judgmental, cheaters, and so on, perhaps there is a generational aspect to those sins that needs to be forgiven and confessed before God's character and nature can be established. Until I discovered the following scriptural principle regarding generational sin found in Leviticus 26:39-42 and applied it, certain sins had such momentum in my life, it seemed impossible to overcome them.

LEVITICUS 26:39-42

"Those of you who are left will waste away in the lands of their enemies because of their sins; also because of their fathers' sins they will waste away. But, if they will confess their sins and the sins of their fathers—their treachery against me and their hostility toward me, which made me hostile toward them so that I sent them into the land of their enemies—then when their uncircumcised hearts are humbled and they pay for their sin, I will remember my covenant with Jacob and my covenant with Isaac and my covenant with Abraham, and I will remember the land."

In verse 39 it says *"those of you who are left will waste away in the lands of their enemies."* Obviously, some in the generations being addressed have already died in their sins and their father's sins. *"Waste away"* means that there is a lack of flourishing; want and need is characteristic of their lives. *"Lands of their enemies"* in this scripture refers to the physical enemies of Israel as a nation. The *"lands"* of our enemies include addiction, abuse, rejection, abandonment, materialism, greed, sexual sin and perversion, lust for power, control, and a large variety of other strongholds. These strongholds can be, or have been passed down, from one generation to the next.

"...because of their sins; also because of their fathers' sins they will waste away." In the previous 38 verses of Leviticus 26, God had been trying to turn His people back to godly ways and away from the sins that had been going on for generations. The Israelites knew the laws and principles of God. However, just like with us today, if dad and/or mom don't "walk the talk," their children are more apt to follow their walk than their talk. This pattern of sin and rebellion seldom gets weaker as it goes from one generation to the other. Quite the contrary, it usually gets stronger.

If their fathers had confessed their sins and the sins of the previous generations, they would have reaped the benefits of obedience and passed those benefits on to the next generation. *"But if they will confess their sins and the sins of their fathers—their treachery against me and their hostility toward me, which made me hostile toward them so that I sent them into the land of their enemies—...."* (Lev. 26:40-41)

To break the power of generational sin, we not only have to confess our sin, but the sins of our fathers. How have we, and previous generations, been treacherous and hostile towards God? If you have already recognized some of the sins mentioned earlier as being in your family, then you know where to begin. Here are some steps we have followed to apply this scripture:

- Father, forgive me for my sin of being critical and judgmental.

- I forgive my mother, her mother, and her mother's mother for this generational sin pattern or stronghold.

- I ask that You would cleanse me from every trace and remnant of these sins and establish the mind of Christ in me.

- I take authority, in Jesus' Name, over this stronghold and order it to depart from me and my family line.

- Father, replace this critical spirit with Your love. Help me to see others through Your eyes of love, forgiveness and mercy.

These instructions are rather simplified but are intended to be an example of how to start dealing with generational sin. God is not a formula God. God is concerned with your heart. Praying from a heart that desires to be more like Jesus will accomplish more than reciting our prayers. You don't have to follow our prayer pattern, but do follow the scriptural pattern He gives you in His Word.

If you don't want to change, God will allow you to stay where you are. He doesn't stop loving you. However, it may be a little more difficult for Him to release His blessings into your life. The blessings will be contaminated with pride, self-righteousness, and other attitude issues. Not only that, your children will suffer in the land of their enemies (if they aren't already) because of your sins, and the sins of your fathers. God's mercies are new every morning, but if you don't appropriate them by following His scriptural pattern and instructions, they don't do you much good.

"—then when their uncircumcised hearts are humbled and they pay for their sin..." (Lev. 26:41) This whole process of confessing our father's sins as our own can create anger in people, especially those who have been abandoned or abused by their parents or other authority figures. When the Lord began to show my husband the generational aspect of lying, he told the Lord, "But if You hadn't given me such a liar for a father, I wouldn't have learned to lie so well." He didn't realize that once he lied the first time and every time thereafter, he became just like his father! Instead of owning his own deceptive nature, he tried to **excuse, blame, justify** and **deny** that it was his fault. (There are those four words again!) In fact, it was God's fault for giving him such a liar for a father.

An uncircumcised heart is one that has too much flesh

(pride) and not enough God. True humility will admit to your sin, confess it, and forgive others who sinned against you. After doing this, we can accept the payment Christ made for our sins on the cross. His is the only blood sacrifice that will atone for our sins. We really believe that when we begin to follow this scriptural pattern of repentance for generational sin, God will reverse the curses in our family line. We also believe that, as we deal with the generational sin the Holy Spirit reveals to us, our families will begin to walk in God's blessings. Psalm 103:17-18 says, *"But from everlasting to everlasting the Lord's love is with those who fear him, and his righteousness with their children's children—with those who keep his covenant and remember to obey his precepts."*

I had a sin pattern I developed growing up, which I managed to pass on to some of my children, so I call it first generation sin. In other words, to my knowledge I was the first generation of this sin or iniquity and my children became the second.

I was always a sulky, pouty child. I carried these traits into my marriage. The Lord began to speak to me one day about giving these traits up. I argued with Him, citing the fact that I had always been this way. Therefore, He must have created me like this. How could He expect me to change when He created me this way? It was unfair!

Have you ever won an argument with God? I haven't. Fortunately, though, He was always patient with me as I explained to Him why He was being unreasonable. When I completed my explanation, He simply said, "But I did not give you a downcast spirit." OH. If He didn't give me these character traits, they must have come from the enemy. The lights went off in my head. With God's help I could change! I repented of my sins and asked God to work this pattern out of my life—and He has. It didn't happen overnight, but I am no longer pouty and sulky.

In a way it was difficult to give up this and other ungodly patterns of behavior, because I got attention through them. It was negative attention, but it was attention, none-the-less. Psalm 66:18 says, *"If I had cherished sin in my heart—the Lord would not have listened."* In other words, if I didn't want to change and wanted to hang on to these characteristics, He would have allowed me to. But doing so would have had a detrimental effect on my prayers, present and future.

Sometimes we excuse our anger, sexual sin, stubbornness and other forms of sin because of our cultural heritage. But as a born-again child of God, we are to conform to our Heavenly Father's character and nature. Our bodies may have come from, for example, Irish, German or other heritage, but we no longer have to carry the ungodly characteristics found in our bloodline. The psalmist must have confessed his sin because he goes on to say in Psalm 66: 19-20, "*but God has surely listened and heard my voice in prayer. Praise be to God, who has not rejected my prayer or withheld his love from me!*"

SCRIPTURAL UNDERSTANDING

In Isaiah 53:5 we are told, "*But he was pierced for our transgressions, he was crushed for our iniquities; the punishment that brought us peace was upon him, and by his wounds we are healed.*" When Jesus was pierced (or wounded), there was an outward shedding of blood. The piercing or outward shedding of blood was for our transgressions or sin. Crushing or bruising causes an inward shedding of blood. The inward shedding of blood that Christ suffered was for our iniquities. Our iniquities are the sins that come out of our inward, sinful nature. This is the nature that we inherited from our ancestors.

My nature was critical and judgmental, just like the natures of my mother and grandmother. My husband's father lied a lot. My husband lied a lot. My nature was unforgiving and twisted with self-pity, as was my father's. My husband and I didn't want to be the way we were; however, we were naturally that way because our natures were inherited generationally. We have found that in order to take on the character and nature of Christ, we have to deal with both our sins (outward behaviors) and our iniquity (inward nature). Examples:

- "Father, forgive me for lying. I forgive my father and past generations for their deceptive natures. My very nature is a liar. Cleanse me from this deceptive nature and establish me in Your Truth."

- "Father, forgive me for being so judgmental and critical. I forgive my mother and past generations for their critical and judgmental natures. My very nature is critical and judgmental. Cleanse my nature and establish me in Your Truth, mercy, and compassion."

- "Father, forgive me for bitterness and unforgiveness. I forgive my father and past generations for this iniquity. My very nature is unforgiving and polluted with bitterness. Cleanse my nature and establish in me Your nature of mercy and compassion."

If you feel stuck in some sin, you don't have to sit around being angry at yourself or God. You can come out of those areas of sin by applying His Word and principles to them. **His Word works if you work His Word!** You will never become accomplished using a gift or talent if you don't practice. It's the same with the Word of God. Practice, practice, practice. *"Let us not become weary in doing good, for at the proper time we will reap a harvest if we do not give up."* (Galatians 6:9)

God's people truly are destroyed from a lack of knowledge. We are told in Hosea 4:6, *"—my people are destroyed from lack of knowledge. Because you have rejected knowledge, I also reject you as priests; because you have ignored the law of your God I also will ignore your children."* If you don't want to follow God for your own peace and joy, do it for your children, so God won't ignore them. Bless your children and your children's children by acting in obedience to the Lord's principles today.

CHAPTER EIGHT

THE ROBE OF RIGHTEOUSNESS

When I was about nine or ten years old, my mom took all four of us girls down to a local department store to buy us new dresses. The store was having a "Going Out of Business" sale, and were selling dresses for fifty cents. With two older sisters, I got many hand-me-downs to wear, so it was a little unusual for me to get a new dress. Many times my mom rewarded good behavior with something new. I had not done anything recently worthy of a reward, so this was doubly special to me.

While I tried on the dresses, my mom commented to me that I looked like a princess in one of them. I was really surprised by her comment, because I thought I was the ugliest thing that walked the face of the earth. When we got home I went to my room and daydreamed about being Cinderella.

I thought my mom must really love me, because she had bought me three new dresses and I had done nothing to deserve them.

When I went out into the kitchen later, she asked me if I had emptied the garbage. I told her, "no," not meaning I wouldn't, just meaning that I hadn't yet done that chore. Her response was, "Those dresses can go right back to the store, if you don't obey."

I was devastated. Her love for me and my worth and value were based on performance. It was like a knife had gone through my heart. She must have had no idea of the negative impact those words had on me; otherwise, I don't believe she would have ever said them. They were death words to me. *"The tongue has the power of life and death..."* (Proverbs 18:21a)

I remembered this incident numerous times after I was saved and had forgiven my mom. However, my soul was still wounded, and when this memory came back again I began to weep. I couldn't understand why I would still be hurting from this incident after so many years, and after forgiving my mom. But, you see, it was the little girl who was wounded, and the little girl needed healing.

The Lord showed me His presence in the memory.

Together we took out the garbage. He held my hand as we walked back into the kitchen. When we saw my mom sitting at the counter, He stopped and looked at me. He then looked at my mom and back at me. He did this three times. The third time He looked at me and smiled. I knew it was the little girl who needed to forgive her mother, and I did.

Jesus and I went back into my bedroom and I remember crying very hard. He held me and let me cry. He showed me later that those tears were an outward expression of the deep grief and mourning I had in my soul because of the "death words" spoken to me. He let me get that sorrow out of my soul without criticizing me. In our discomfort over dealing with a child's pain, we sometimes say things like, "Big girls don't cry," or impatiently tell the child to quit crying. Jesus didn't do that. He comforted me in my sorrow by just holding me until my crying ceased.

Jesus then went to my closet and opened the door. He told me to come over and look inside. When I did I saw the most beautiful white dress I had ever seen. It sparkled. It glowed. It was dazzling—and it was mine! Jesus said, "I bought this for you with a price no one else can pay. I bought it for you with My blood." Mom paid fifty cents for my Cinderella dress. Jesus paid the ultimate price for my robe of righteousness. I didn't have to earn it. When I saw that dress, my soul was healed. I no longer carry the hurt of that memory, because the presence of Jesus healed me.

Several months later we were teaching a ministry training class at the church we attended. We taught on emotional healing, and I shared this experience with the class. Many of the people in the class were healed of childhood wounds. We went into the sanctuary and when the worship began, I raised my hands in worship and thanksgiving to the Lord for what He has done for me. In the midst of worship, He spoke to my heart. He said, "Judy, I gave you that dress three months ago and you have never put it on."

He was right, of course. Whenever I thought of this healing experience, my mind would go back to the closet and just stand in awe of the beautiful dress Jesus had given me. It never occurred to me to put it on. I knew that as a little girl, the dress was too big for me. It was too big then, but when I was in my 30's and experienced the saving love of Jesus, it fit me perfectly. Jesus apparently thought it was time for me to wear it. As I continued to worship, it was as if the Lord Himself slipped that dress over my upraised arms. I received and was adorned in this beautiful gift of His righteousness.

It was at that moment that I could begin to love myself. I

became a beautiful person. Hollywood would probably take issue with that, but it really doesn't matter what other people think. I am beautiful in God's sight. I am His bride. I am robed in the splendor of His holiness. Romans 13:14 tells us to, "*...clothe yourselves with the Lord Jesus Christ...*"

His righteousness is available to us. All we have to do is accept Christ as our personal Savior and Lord. He did all the rest on the cross. The question is, do you know that you can walk in His righteousness? Have you clothed yourself with the Lord Jesus Christ? Your garment was prepared before the foundations of the earth, when He saw your unformed body. "*You knit me together in my mother's womb.*" (Psalm 139:13) "*My frame was not hidden from You when I was made in the secret place. When I was woven together in the depths of the earth, Your eyes saw my unformed body.*" (Psalm 139:15-16b) He chose you to be His closest companion.

It was difficult for me to accept these scriptural truths when my soul was still contaminated with the childhood hurts. But God has His way of cleansing and healing our souls. When we learn about the various ways He can heal us, the tools He has made available, it is then time to use them.

CHAPTER NINE

FORGIVENESS AND UNFORGIVENESS

One of the most important principles we have learned in our Christian walk is the principle and power of forgiveness.

Forgiving others is not a suggestion from God. Forgiving is a command. Jesus said in Matthew 6:14-15: *"For if you forgive men their trespasses, your heavenly Father will also forgive you. But if you forgive not men their trespasses, neither will your Father forgive your trespasses."* When we set our will against our Father's will (His will is to forgive) then His will is set against us. This is not a pleasant thought—to have God's will set against us. Read that passage again if you are having a difficult time believing me. I didn't say it. The Word of God says it.

Forgiving others (and yourself, by the way) will ensure

that you have access to the Father. I held a relative in unforgiveness after a particularly hurtful letter that was sent to me. I kept the letter, and even made copies of it in case the original was lost. I wanted to be certain that I could hold the evidence up and shake it in my relative's face after my relative had accepted Christ. The longer I kept the letter and copies, the harder my heart became. A root of bitterness developed that went down into my soul and came out of my mouth. This bitterness contaminated many. (Hebrews 12:15) Roots of bitterness only grow in rocky soil poisoned with unforgiveness. When I was finally able to forgive and then burned the letter and copies, my heart condition changed and God gave me His love for this relative.

I used the age-old excuse to hold on to my anger and unforgiveness by saying that I would forgive when my relative asked for forgiveness. Christ was never asked by the world if He would forgive before He went to the cross. Just the opposite was true. From the cross He asked the Father to forgive them (us). His example is the one we are to follow.

Sometimes I used the excuse that I wasn't done being mad yet. I would forgive after I cooled down. There is no evidence that Jesus had to have a cool down period before He forgave. Forgiving begins with a choice to line my heart up with the Word of God. Jesus said to forgive, so I make the choice. My feelings will follow as long as I continue to make the choice to keep my heart right with the Father.

There were other times when I just wanted the offender to suffer before I forgave. If I forgave too soon, he or she might think they could get away with hurting me again. Forgiving others is for your own benefit. The offender may never know how much they hurt you, but by forgiving without being asked, you will be able to hear from the Holy Spirit how to deal with the offender and offense. You can be healed. **Forgiveness is the key that unlocks the door for your healing.**

Perhaps you have noticed that I used "excuses" to avoid dealing with my sin. In the process of excusing myself, I put the requirement on the other person to ask for forgiveness before I would extend it. I justified my unscriptural position by the degree of hurt I suffered. I denied that I was at fault in any way and, basically, blamed the other person for my unforgiveness. If they hadn't done what they did and hurt me so bad, I wouldn't be struggling with this! I think we have heard these four words before—**excuse, blame, justify and deny**! We all do it, but like Jesus said on the cross, they "*do not know what they are doing.*" (Luke 23:34)

At the time, I did not know that I was sinning. I could only see the other person's sin. After all, I was the one who was hurt. I had a right to be angry and expect an apology before I forgave this offense.

We heard a Sunday School teaching in 1982 that I will never forget. The subject was on our rights as Christians. The pastor basically said that, as Christians, we are dead people. We have no rights. That really struck me, because in my heart I had often used the excuse, "I have a right." If I am dead to self and alive in Christ, my selfish rights are dead also. A dead person doesn't have any rights. A dead person cannot be offended. A dead person can only control you beyond the grave if you allow it. If you are dead to your trespasses and sin, you can begin to say "no" to everything it brings up. The old nature lives in the measure we allow it.

We do have one right as Christians—to become like Jesus. I am alive in Him so I have the right to become like Him. That means I have to give my will to the Father and allow God to direct my life. Unfortunately, I was so blinded by my pride and self-righteousness that I couldn't see my own sin.

We haven't found any loopholes in the command to forgive. In Mark 11:25 we are told, *"And when you stand praying, if you hold anything against anyone, forgive him, so that your Father in heaven may forgive you your sins.*" Forgiving others enables the Father to forgive us our sins. It says that your Father is able to forgive you when you forgive others.

We are even commanded to forgive (be reconciled) to our brother if he has something against us. In Matthew 5:23-24 we are told, *"Therefore, if you are offering your gift at the altar and there remember that your brother has something against you, leave your gift there in front of the altar. First go and be reconciled to your brother, then come and offer your gift."* In other words, if you know that someone is offended by something you said or did, even before the individual makes it known to you, as a Christian it is your responsibility to go to him or her and seek forgiveness and healing.

The parable of the unmerciful servant is found in Matthew 18:21-35. It is a sobering reminder of the consequences of unforgiveness. Verses 32-35 tell us, *"Then the master called the servant in. 'You wicked servant,' he said, 'I canceled all that debt of yours because you begged me to. Shouldn't you have had mercy on your fellow servant just as I had on you?' In anger his master **turned him over to the jailers to be tortured**, until he should pay back all he owed. This is how my heavenly Father will treat each of you unless you forgive* *your brother from your heart.*" [Emphasis added.]

Forgiveness begins in our minds with a choice to obey the Word of God. Each offense can become a layer of unforgiveness. In order for forgiveness to complete its work in our hearts, we have to be willing to forgive every layer of offense that the Holy Spirit uncovers. If forgiveness doesn't get into our hearts, we can still suffer torment and pain from the offense.

The tormentors mentioned in Matthew 18:32-35 will have no room to operate when you are able to forgive all offenses and offenders. However, that is only the first step. When you have held unforgiveness in your heart, you have sinned. Unforgiveness is sin. If you find the Holy Spirit prompting you to forgive someone, it means you have held unforgiveness in your heart. Unforgiveness is the offended party's sin. It is not the sin of the offender. If you are the offended party, it is time to forgive and to be forgiven.

Unforgiveness is the first sin in a series of six that I want to outline for your cleansing and healing. First John 1:9 says, "*If we confess our **sins**, he is faithful and just and will forgive us our sins and purify us from all unrighteousness.*" Admit your sin of unforgiveness, confess it to God and He will forgive you.

CHAPTER TEN

JUDGING

The second sin in the series is judging. In Luke 6:37 Jesus says, *"Do not judge, and you will not be judged. Do not condemn, and you will not be condemned. Forgive, and you will be forgiven."* In Matthew 7:1-2 He says, *"Do not judge, or you too will be judged. For in the same way you judge others, you will be judged, and with the measure you use, it will be measured to you."*

I judged my mother that she didn't love me, wouldn't protect me, and I couldn't trust her. These were not intentional judgments, but when I realized that I had indeed judged my mother in these ways, I had to repent of my sin. Judgments are sin. Everybody does it, but that doesn't make it right according to the scriptures quoted above. Unintentional sin is addressed in numerous places in the

Bible. For instance, Leviticus 4:27-28 says, "*If a member of the community sins unintentionally and does what is forbidden in any of the Lord's commands, he is guilty. When he is made aware of the sin he committed, he must bring as his offering for the sin he committed a female goat without defect.*" Unintentional sins will not keep us out of heaven. However, when we learn of unintentional sins, we need to confess them and get them cleansed.

The common form that judgments take are the names we call people or words we use to describe our opinion of them. By the way, opinions you have of others that are negative and demeaning, are really judgments.

Judgments can be specific: "My wife always has to have things her way;" "My husband is so wishy-washy, I have to make all the important decisions;" "My boss is a total jerk;" " I am so stupid" (worthless, no good, etc.). Judgments can be against others and against yourself.

Judgments can also be all-inclusive: "No man can be trusted;" "Women always try to dominate and control me;" "Women are airheads who run on emotions;" "All cops (IRS, military, school authorities, church authorities, etc.), are jerks." When we see all of a particular group or class of people through the eyes of the judgments we hold them in, we are guilty of all-inclusive judgments. Family feuds, bigotry, racial prejudices that go from generation to generation began in judgments.

We had a gentleman in a class we conducted years ago who came forward for ministry following the teaching on forgiveness. He said he hated all law enforcement officials. In his opinion there wasn't one good cop in the county he lived in, and probably in the whole state. We questioned him about this hatred and found out when it began to pollute his life. He and his wife were on the verge of divorce because his bitterness was infecting their relationship. We took him through forgiveness of the police officers who handled the domestic violence call his wife had made seven years earlier. We took him through forgiveness of his wife and daughter, and then had him repent of his unforgiveness, judgments, revenge, and inner vows he had made as a result of this incident. He also had to repent of dishonoring his wife and authority, as well as dishonoring God. We will cover those sins shortly. We then prayed for his heart to be healed from the effects of his sin.

The next week he and his wife came to class beaming with joy. The roots of bitterness had been cleansed by repentance and forgiveness. Their relationship had begun the journey to healing. As long as he didn't see his own sins and repent of them, he remained bound in judgments, revenge, and bitterness. It was impossible for him to see those he previously judged the way God saw them. He was looking at all law enforcement through the lens of unforgiveness and bitterness. Time for a new prescription. The new prescription included forgiveness and repentance. Repentance is a gift from God. Acts 11:18 says, *"So then, God has even granted [given as a free gift] the Gentiles repentance unto life."* Receive and use this gift. It brings cleansing, healing and freedom.

Judgments can be against God also. I judged God to be the "Great Scorekeeper in the Sky." As long as I viewed Him that way I couldn't see Him for who He is—my loving, gracious Heavenly Father. Judgments against God will limit His ability to move in our lives and in the lives of others. Mark 6:1-6 is a scriptural example of this.

" Jesus left there and went to his hometown, accompanied by his disciples. When the Sabbath came, he began to teach in the synagogue, and many who heard him were amazed.

"Where did this man get these things?" they asked. "What's this wisdom that has been given him, that he even

does miracles! Isn't this the carpenter? Isn't this Mary's son and the brother of James, Joseph, Judas and Simon? Aren't his sisters here with us?" And they took offense at him.

Jesus said to them, 'Only in his hometown, among his relatives and in his own house is a prophet without honor.' He could not do any miracles there, except lay his hands on a few sick people and heal them. And he was amazed at their lack of faith."

Jesus' home town was where He grew up. The people knew Him when He was a little boy and a fellow classmate at the synagogue. They knew his family whom they considered ordinary people. He was just a carpenter. They responded to His teaching and ministry with envy and jealousy, which led to judgments and offense. "Who does He think He is? He comes into town like a bigshot and know-it-all. We had the same teachers He had. What makes Him think He is so wise that He can tell us what to do? He's just a carpenter. We don't have to listen to Him."

This is the same kind of attitude that Moses faced in Numbers 12:1-2, *"Miriam and Aaron began to talk against Moses because of his Cushite wife, for he had married a Cushite. 'Has the Lord spoken only through Moses?' they asked. 'Hasn't he also spoken through us?' And the Lord heard this."*

"Who does Moses think he is? He isn't the only person on earth who has heard from God. He married a Cushite. How can God actually use him?"

"Only in his hometown, among his relatives and in his own house is a prophet without honor." (Mark 6:4) The judgments that the people held against Jesus limited his ability to minister—*"He could not do any miracles there, except lay his hands on a few sick people and heal them."* (Mark 6:5) When we have judgments against God, it will affect His ability to heal and do other miracles in our lives. Our judgments will affect the spiritual atmosphere in whatever meeting we are attending, whether it is a church service, evangelistic gathering or healing service. "I know the Bible says Jesus healed, but He has never healed me. I'll just wait until I see for myself before I'll believe." Thomas had to see to believe—so do I. God will have to prove Himself to me. After all, this is no big name TV evangelist who is proclaiming that God heals. This is just my pastor."

"And He was amazed at their lack of faith." Judgments against God are like filters through which we view Him and those that come proclaiming the Good News. Judgments against God will kill or severely limit your faith. When you

recognize judgments you hold against God, confess the judgments as sin and ask God to forgive you. Then ask Him to help you understand the truth about His character and nature and to build up your faith. You don't want to limit God, do you? Free Him from the binding judgments you have and release Him to move freely in and through you, making you a vessel fit for the King.

CHAPTER ELEVEN

REVENGE AND INNER VOWS

R evenge is the third level of sin for which an offended party needs to repent. *"Do not take revenge, my friends, but leave room for God's wrath, for it is written: 'It is mine to avenge; I will repay,' says the Lord."* (Romans 12:19) He didn't give revenge to anyone. It is His exclusively. He may use a person or people group to work His vengeance on the disobedient, but only His prophets knew who these instruments of vengeance were. When vengeance becomes our decision, then we have taken into our own hands something that belongs exclusively to God.

The Lord brought this sin to my awareness through a revelation He gave me. I was pondering on the scripture about vengeance being God's, and He spoke to my heart that I had acted in vengeance towards my husband and others. I was horrified to think that I could have committed this sin. I saw revenge as intentionally hurting others through words, attitudes and actions. The ultimate revenge is murder. I hadn't intentionally taken revenge out on anyone—well, not as bad as other people I knew who deliberately acted in revenge, or so I thought.

The Lord asked me how I acted when I was upset with my husband. I thought about the times I had slammed cupboard doors, stormed through the house, and shut him out of my heart. These were acts of revenge! I couldn't hit him (as I felt like doing) but I could let him know I was mad in subtle (and not-so-subtle) ways and then make him pay a price by emotionally isolating myself from him for a few days. My knees went weak as I realized how my unforgiveness and judgments led into the sin of revenge.

In a courtroom, a judge has a legal right to determine if a person is guilty, or, in other words, to judge the individual. If guilty, the judge has a right and obligation to determine the price the violator has to pay for violating the law, either in cash or time. God's children were not given the right to judge others or to extract a price from our offenders. That is God's job exclusively. We can judge if certain behaviors are sin and address those sins, but we do not have the right to judge and extract revenge on the sinner.

In the revelation I saw the throne room of God. He was seated on the throne and beside the throne was a gold box inscribed with the words, "God's Property." Someone came into the throne room, thumbed his nose at God, marched over to the box, picked it up and marched out of the throne room. God showed me that in the box was revenge. When I act in revenge, it is the same as marching into His throne room, thumbing my nose at Him, taking His property and then marching out. "Vengeance is Mine," saith the Lord. It is not mine. It is not yours. It belongs exclusively to God.

When I researched revenge in the Bible, I found that it has a boomerang effect. If we take revenge into our own hands, then the same thing we are doing to others will come back on us. Sometimes we pray that God will take revenge on others for us. We have to be really careful, because these prayers are usually motivated by unforgiveness and judgments.

Inner vows are the next level of sin that has to be recognized and for which we must repent. Inner vows (or oaths) are thoughtless or careless promises you make to yourself. They are unintentional sin. Leviticus 5:4-5 says, *"Or if a person thoughtlessly takes an oath to do anything whether good or evil—in any matter one might carelessly swear*

about—even though he is unaware of it, in any case when he learns of it he will be guilty. When anyone is guilty in any of these ways, he must confess in what way he has sinned..."
Here are examples of inner vows that are commonly made:

- I will never be like my mother.
- I will never be like my father.
- I will never treat my kids the way my parents treated me.
- I will never be an alcoholic.
- I will never let a man hurt me again.
- I will never let a woman control me.
- I will never be without money when I grow up.
- Nobody will tell me what to do when I grow up.
- I will be the strong one—I will never cry again.

Whatever form these inner vows have taken, they are sin according to the above quote from Leviticus 5:4-5.

Inner vows are promises we make to ourselves that seem good at the time. They are usually not intentional sin. In fact, the scripture said, *"even though he is unaware of it."* I told myself I would never treat my children the way my mom treated me. This inner vow was based on my judgments of my mother. Do you know that you cannot get good fruit from a bad tree? (Matthew 17:17) Inner vows (*whether for good or evil*) are based on unforgiveness, judgments and revenge. Good fruit will not grow from those vows.

We had a man take exception to this teaching. He was furious to think that the promise he made to himself that he would never treat his children the way his father treated him could be wrong. His father physically abused the family. He swore he would never hit his children and he never had! How could that be sin? His father was the sinner!

It is his sin, because the Word of God says inner vows are sin. It is sin because his vow was based on unforgiveness and judgments he held against his father. Even though this man had never hit his children, he went to the opposite extreme from the way his father parented and did not apply appropriate discipline and establish boundaries for his children. Neither extreme produced good fruit. The last we heard, one of this man's children entered into an ungodly sexual lifestyle. The other became rebellious and began using drugs. The point is, inner vows, whether made for good or evil purposes, do not produce good fruit. They will bind you into behavior patterns that you know are contrary to the Word of God, because you promised yourself you would never be that way.

If you realize now that you have had judgments, revenge

and inner vows against your parents, repent and get those sins cleansed. Then ask God to pattern you after the character and nature of Christ. Overcome evil with good. Go from, "I never want to be like my father and/or mother," to "God, I want to be like You."

When I learned of the inner vows I had made, I had to repent of them and break the power they held over me and my relationship with my mother. The first weekend after doing this, we visited my folks. We arrived about 9:30 p.m. When I walked into the dimly lit entry, my mom looked at my face and said, "What did you do to your face? Your face is different. What did you do to your face?" I had been carrying the unforgiveness, judgments and inner vows on my countenance. She saw the difference. I knew my heart was different towards my mom, but I didn't realize it would be manifest on my face.

From the time I repented of my own sin against my mother, I was able to love her with God's love. She did have a critical spirit, and continued to operate in that generational stronghold. However, I didn't have to take her critical remarks into my heart. Now my shield of faith and breastplate of righteousness were working. Prior to the recognition and repentance of my own sin, I thought if mom would only change I wouldn't get hurt by her critical words. My sins of unforgiveness, judgments and inner vows had caused my breastplate

> Sin, (unrighteousness) puts a hole in your breastplate of righteousness

of righteousness to have a big hole in it. The unrighteousness of sin created that hole. Repentance sealed over the hole and whatever fiery darts of criticism that were fired no longer found a target. And I thought my mom had to change before I could really love her. Wrong! I had to change.

Another interesting note to this story is that I was able to become an adult in my relationship with my mom. She no longer controlled me with guilt and fear. I stopped responding like a little girl around her, afraid that I would disappoint her or make her angry if I didn't do everything the way she wanted and when she wanted. Recognition, ownership of my own sin, followed by repentance, brought the freedom I needed.

CHAPTER TWELVE

DISHONORING PEOPLE
AND DISHONORING GOD

Dishonoring of People. There are many ways you can dishonor people but we will focus on the following three: 1) dishonoring of parents, 2) dishonoring of spouse, and 3) dishonoring of authorities.

Exodus 20:12 says, *"Honor your father and mother, so that you may live long in the land."* Notice the scripture does not say to honor parents IF they act honorably. An unfortunate number of adults have been abused by parents—verbally, emotionally, physically, or sexually. How in the world do you honor a person who has used, abused, neglected, abandoned and/or rejected you? First you have to forgive the offender. After forgiving, you deal with your own sins of unforgiveness, judgments, revenge, inner vows and dishonoring. When your sins are confessed and forgiven, ask God to give you His love for the parent (or step-parent) Ask God to give you wisdom to know if you are to have a relationship with the parent. God does not want any of His children to be a doormat for abuse in any relationship. Malachi 2:16 says, *"'I hate divorce,' says the Lord God of Israel, 'and I hate a man's covering himself with violence as well as with his garments.'"* We usually hear the first part of that scripture quoted but the second half of it is just as important: God hates violence in a relationship as much as He hates divorce. He also hates a person trying to cover his sin with the garments of excusing, blaming, justifying and denying. Individuals who are in an abusive relationship do not have to stay there. However, you may find that after forgiving and repenting, God's love will take things in a new direction. Get your heart right and find out where things will go. As my heart became right with God, before my mom died we were closer than we had ever been.

Ephesians 5:33 tells us that, *"each one of you also must love his wife as he loves himself, and the wife must respect her husband."* Husbands, if you are not loving your wife as you love yourself (and as Christ loved the church) you are not honoring her. When you hold her in unforgiveness, judgments, revenge and inner vows, it is impossible to love her the way God intends. Wives, if you are holding your husband in unforgiveness, judgments, revenge, and inner vows, you are not respecting him, or the divine order that Christ established for the home. Your dishonoring attitude will make it impossible to submit to his leadership.

Many Christian homes are out of order. The woman tends to be the head, if not in every area, at least in the spiritual realm. Obeying the precepts in God's Word is your primary responsibility. If your husband wants you to violate God's commands by doing things that go against your conscience and knowledge of the Word, then you are obliged to follow God.

I was only saved about a year when the Lord asked me to submit to my husband. My protest sounded something like this: "God, You can't be serious! How do I follow a blind man?" God said, "How did you learn the lessons I have taught you?" I replied, "By the mistakes I have made." He said, "I want you to give him the same grace I gave you when you made mistakes, because that is how I am going to teach him some of the lessons he will learn."

I again protested, "But God, he is the leader. If he falls in a ditch, we all fall in a ditch. That's not fair! Why should

I pay a price for his sin?" God said ever-so-gently, "In that case, I am your covering, I will protect you."

I learned that my trust and submission had to be to God first, then to the position in which He put my husband. It was difficult to learn how to submit and honor Eldon as head of the home. He had never functioned as the head except when he wanted to do something that I didn't want. Then he was the head—he did what he wanted.

When I finally submitted in my heart and stopped arguing in my head, I was twice-covered—by the Lord and by my husband. It took Eldon a few years to grow into the godly head of our home. It took me a few years to adapt to this new role but now God's divine order has been established in our home. We live in peace with one another.

When we hold authorities in unforgiveness, judgments, revenge and inner vows, we are not honoring them. Romans 13:1-2, *"Everyone must submit himself to the governing authorities, for there is no authority except that which God has established. The authorities that exist have been established by God. Consequently, he who rebels against the authority is rebelling against what God has instituted, and those who do so will bring judgment."*

Many of us feel that if we don't agree with an authority,

then we don't have to honor the person who is in authority. However, if God established all authority as the above scripture indicates, then our attitude towards the authority must be one of honor. We don't have to agree with everything that the authority says and does, but every authority has been established by God. Verse 5 says, *"Therefore, it is necessary to submit to the authorities, not only because of possible punishment but also because of conscience."*

In Acts 4:19 Peter and John give the scriptural position we can all take when authorities tell us to do, or not do, something that contradicts God's principles and law. "But Peter and John replied, *'Judge for yourselves whether it is right in God's sight to obey you rather than God. For we cannot help speaking about what we have seen and heard.'*" The disciples had a direct command from Jesus Himself to, *"Go into all the world and preach the good news to all creation."* (Mark 16:15) As Christians, our first loyalty is to the Word of God. When authority tells us to violate the Word, then we obey the Word and not the authority.

After Nathan the prophet confronted David with his sin, David said in Psalm 51:4, *"Against you and you only have I sinned, O Lord, and done what is evil in your sight..."*

David sinned against many people when he committed

adultery with Bathsheba, but he realized that all his sins were ultimately against God. All his sins hurt the heart of his Heavenly Father and he dishonored God with his sin. Romans 2:23, *"You who brag about the law, do you dishonor God by breaking the law?"*

To briefly recap this information, it is not up to the offender to change before you deal with your own sin. The six sins I outlined beginning in Chapter 9 include:

1. Unforgiveness
2. Judgments
3. Revenge
4. Inner vows
5. Dishonoring or parents/spouse/authorities
6. Dishonoring God.

To be like Jesus, we forgive others when they sin against us. We then ask God to forgive us for our own sins.

CHAPTER THIRTEEN

MY JOURNEY CONTINUED

Several years ago an evangelist visited our church. I wasn't particularly impressed with his appearance (oops—a judgment) but he had some really good things to say. One night a friend of his who was in the audience asked if he could sing part of a song that was on his heart. It wasn't a hymn verse, but he felt like the Holy Spirit was prompting him to sing it. When he did, I knew it was for me. He sang, "Don't sit under the apple tree with anyone else but me, with anyone else but me, with anyone else but me. Don't sit under the apple tree with anyone else but me." I don't remember just how that chorus ended but those words ministered to my heart.

For years prior to this I would get up in the middle of the night when I couldn't sleep and spend time with the Lord.

The night after the "apple tree" song was sung, I was again up in the middle of the night, sitting in my chair with my Bible open on my lap. My spirit was opened to see myself sitting under that apple tree waiting for Jesus, my Beloved, to come—and He did! I saw Jesus approach me with His hand extended and a smile on His face. He sat beside me and together we read His Word. He explained things to me that I hadn't understood before. He laughed about some of the things the disciples did, and we just enjoyed each other's company. This went on every night for months. I knew, and know, that He is my Beloved and I am His.

Several days later the speaker told us to go home and ask Jesus to give us a "love letter." He said to get quiet before the Lord, and ask Him to tell us how much He loves us and to write what He says down.

I was not convinced that I would hear clearly enough to get a "love letter" from Jesus; but, because it was an assignment, I had to try. I didn't want to be embarrassed the next day when he asked who did their assignment.

I knew from experience that Jesus would meet me under the apple tree in the middle of the night, but I wasn't sure if mid-afternoon was a good time for Him! Never-the-less, I got a notepad and put myself in a place of receiving whatever

He wanted to say. I then began to write. Jesus did give me a love letter from His heart. I kept it to myself for years. It was so personal and amazing to me that I didn't want to share it with anyone else. The evangelist asked for everyone to turn in their love letter the next day but I wouldn't part with mine, or even share a copy at that point.

Several years later, the Holy Spirit impressed me to give a copy to a young woman who was in an identity crisis— she didn't feel loved by anyone. The letter really ministered to her. Since that initial time of sharing this very personal love letter, the Lord has had me share it with many others. I believe He wants me to share it with the readers of this book also. We are all the bride of Christ. This is a love letter to His Bride, to you.

My Darling Bride,

How do I love thee? Let me count the ways.

I have had my eye on you before creation. I pointed you out to My Father as you were being formed in your mother's womb and I told Him that I wanted you for My very own—that I wanted to spend eternity with you as I have an endless measure of love to lavish upon you. I can never get enough of you.

I love your eyes. They are the windows to a soul so pure and lovely that I never tire of gazing into them. Your soul to Me is like a precious gem that I delight in shaping to reflect the radiance of My love; a gem whose many facets have yet to be discovered. All of them will increase My glory and My presence as they are uncovered and refined. Not only do you have beauty that already takes My breath away, but your yet unrevealed beauty staggers My imagination and brings ecstasy to My heart.

I love you, My bride, with a love impossible to express in words, so I have put My Spirit in you (as a husband deposits his seed within his wife) to conceive, and reveal, and grow within you the fullness of My love. For you see, I see Myself in you!

Your Savior and the lover of your soul,

Jesus

As a part of the Body of Christ, this letter is an expression of His love to you. He has put His Holy Spirit as a deposit in you. Second Corinthians 1:22 says, *"...and put His Spirit in our hearts as a deposit, guaranteeing what is to come."* He expects this deposit to produce new life within you, a life led by the Holy Spirit. Romans 8:14 says, *"because those who are led by the Spirit of God are sons of God."*

Several years after I had first given the letter to someone else, I noticed that Jesus started the letter with "My Darling Bride." I knew He was talking to me when I wrote it, but He didn't have me write "Dear Judy" or "My Darling Judy." Another thing I noticed was that there was no date on it. This is contrary to my usual practice when I receive something memorable from the Lord—I always put the date on it. But the letter is timeless. It is for yesterday, today and forever. It is always applicable to every person who believes in Jesus. He loves you and me with a passionate love. He is anxiously waiting for the time when His Father will tell Him—Son, go get your bride! We, the Church, are the bride of Christ. The word "bride" is not gender specific. It refers to both man and woman. One day we will be with Him in heaven, but while we are on Earth, He wants to have a spiritual relationship that is so close, you will never feel disconnected from His love—ever. This letter will be spiritual food which will nourish your spirit. I pray that it will minister to you with the same impact that it had on me. It is for you.

CHAPTER FOURTEEN

INTO THE THRONE ROOM

I continued to meet with Jesus, My Beloved, every night under the apple tree. One night, as we were sitting together, Jesus got up and told me to come with Him. He said that He wanted to introduce me to His Father. I knew in my heart that this was the equivalent of a young man finding the woman he wanted to marry, and introducing her to his family. I got up and took His arm. Together we entered into the throne room of His Father.

I have no words to describe the throne room other than it was transparent gold glowing with the presence of the Father. It was beauty beyond any imaginable earthly experience. Jesus introduced me to His Father and His Father smiled at me as Jesus told Him this was the woman He wanted to marry. This was His bride.

Then Jesus excused Himself and left momentarily. The Father said to me, "Now, there is someone I want to introduce to you." At that moment, Jesus appeared again, but this time He was robed in royal splendor. His presence was beyond radiant. Again, it is really indescribable. Then the Father said to me, "I want you to meet My Son."

The one who came to me under the apple tree as my friend, my betrothed and the lover of my soul, was actually the King of Kings and the Lord of Lords! When he came to me under the apple tree, He was clothed in pure white garments. Now He was clothed in His royal robes, shining in His radiant light. I fell on my knees before Him and before the Father. Who was I to be worthy to be a part of the family of God? In myself, I am not worthy of such an honor. But, because He loves me and wants me for His own throughout eternity, I am His bride. He is the lover of my soul. I am worthy because He loves me.

I have known the Father and the Son, as well as the Holy Spirit, since 1977. But this precious experience was so profoundly intimate, personal and awesome, that it brings me to tears when I consider the depth of love Jesus has for His bride. He is proud of His bride, the Church. He longs for quiet moments together with her. He loves to bring her to His Father. He longs for the day when He can bring her home forever.

At an evening service in July of 2004, the Lord gave me this word for His people:

Prepare your hearts, My beloved, for I am coming soon. Make your heart pure, as I am coming for My bride. Prepare, adorn yourself with the jewels of my love and peace and joy. Wear the robe of righteousness I have given you. It is your bridal gown. Don't ever take it off, for you know not when I am coming. I will keep it spotless, as you walk in obedience and in My love.

My Father will soon be saying, "Son, go get Your bride." My heart is leaping within me in anticipation of that day. Songs of joy fill My heart and echo through the heavens, as I give voice to My love for you. As your praises ascend unto Me, **My songs for you fill the heavens!**

You are My beloved. Prepare your hearts. I am coming soon.

Imagine the delight that Jesus takes in His bride. Make Him your delight. Isaiah 61:10: "*I delight greatly in the*

Lord; my soul rejoices in my God. For He has clothed me with garments of salvation and arrayed me in a robe of righteousness. As a bridegroom adorns his head like a priest, and as a bride adorns herself with her jewels."

Psalm 45:9b, 11-15: "...at your right hand is the royal bride in gold of Ophir. (11) The king is enthralled by your beauty; honor Him, for He is your lord. The Daughter of Tyre will come with a gift, men of wealth will seek your favor. All glorious is the princess within her chamber, her gown is interwoven with gold. In embroidered garments she is led to the king; her virgin companions follow her and are brought to you. They are led in with joy and gladness; they enter the palace of the king."

"The wedding of the Lamb has come, and his bride has made herself ready." Get ready Church! Jesus is coming soon.

CHAPTER FIFTEEN

SEATED IN HEAVENLY PLACES

Several years after my experience with Jesus introducing me to His Father as His beloved, I went through a time of what I now know to be depression. I was tired of teaching our classes but felt that I had to, because Eldon counted on me. I was feeling as if I had always been in the shadow of someone else. I was somebody's daughter, somebody's sister, somebody's wife, somebody's mother, and the other half of a ministry team—but who was I? Who is the woman called Judy and what are her talents, abilities, personality, likes and dislikes?

The dark cloud of depression began to weigh heavy on my soul. I was tired, cranky, and generally unpleasant to be around most of the time. I was also very self-focused and resentful of other people making demands on my emotional, physical and spiritual strength.

One day, as I was reading in Psalm 17:8, *"Keep me as the apple of your eye; hide me in the shadow of your wings,"* The Lord spoke to my heart as I read those words. He said, "You have always been in a shadow, but it's been My shadow, and that is where you belong." I am realizing as I write this, that the desire I had to be close to God when I was young, was actually Him overshadowing me before I knew Him. When His words sank into my spirit, a weight lifted off my shoulders. I no longer had to perform for anybody. I no longer had to meet everybody's expectations. I was free to pursue God. I was free to sit in His presence and not have to jump up every time someone had a request or emergency. I could now discover who I am. The truth is I already knew — but didn't know I knew. I knew I was His bride, but I didn't know I knew that I no longer had to be under anyone else's shadow. I could emerge with a new confidence in Him and in myself.

Jesus told me that He wanted me to see the experience I had with Him when He introduced me to His Father, as a part of the journey, not the destination. He let me know that He wanted me to move on. I protested because I loved that place. I was beginning to feel a little stale there but it was so awesome, I didn't want to leave it. How could anything else even come close to that special moment in the Father's throne room? What would a relationship with Him be like, if it wasn't in that moment?

He again spoke to me and said, "You are to have a relationship with Me from the throne." This was puzzling to me. I knew I belonged beside Jesus on the throne, but didn't understand how to have a relationship with Him from the throne.

I was not certain what to think of this until my husband and I were ministering to a young woman several years later. We knew her background and her pure love for God. I didn't want to just draw on the understanding of her I already had. I had ministered from my own understanding at times in the past. I would forget that I had access to the Father's heart and the mind of Christ so I didn't always expect Him to help me. This time I saw myself seated beside Jesus on the throne. I leaned my head towards His and asked Him what He wanted me to do, and He told me. The Holy Spirit began to guide and direct the words I spoke. We immediately saw the effectiveness of Christ's power and authority as I spoke deliverance and healing to her. I heard the Lord speak to me again and say, "This is what I meant when I said your relationship with Me is to be from the throne."

I had begun to notice months previously that I prayed with increased confidence. I didn't doubt the effectiveness of my prayers and ministry. I didn't pay much attention to this, but was very grateful to the Lord for the change. The moment He spoke about the meaning of "from the throne," I knew that, as a believer and as His bride, I had access to Him whenever I asked. He had given me His full authority and empowered me to do whatever He wanted me to do. I didn't have to spend days, weeks or months in preparation to come into His presence, as Esther had to before entering her husband's throne room. I only had to ask Him for what I needed, as I did in the ministry example cited above, and then be obedient to the directions the Holy Spirit gave to accomplish His will. It is still taking time to get used to the positional authority He has given me.

It is difficult to grasp the understanding that the Father loves me so much that He will share the secrets of His kingdom with me if I ask, seek, and knock for the answers. Can you imagine having the intimacy of a relationship with the governor of your state or the president of your nation that allows you instant access to him or her no matter what is going on? Can you imagine having access to secret information reserved only for the most trusted members of the King's court? That is what you and I have when we believe in Jesus Christ and release our lives to Him. It may take awhile to learn and understand our position and our authority, but we have both as soon as we believe.

Church, it is time to start believing the Word of God. It is time to move into our place of authority, and get on about the Father's business. We are sons and daughters of the Most High God. We are the Bride of Christ. It is staggering to our imaginations to really believe the unconditional, boundless love He has for us, and the position of authority He has given us. But it is true! If you don't believe me, read The Book.

Get ready Church! Jesus is coming soon. Put His Word into practice. Let the Holy Spirit show you the spots, wrinkles and blemishes on your soul. Ask God to forgive you for your sins and cleanse you from all unrighteousness. Receive the robe of righteousness and walk upright before Him. Take your place on the throne with Him. Don't live in the poverty of deception, doubt and unbelief. Live in the truth, faith and righteousness He has provided through His sacrifice on the cross and glorious resurrection.

Get ready Church! Jesus is coming soon.

CPSIA information can be obtained at www.ICGtesting.com
Printed in the USA
BVOW021904220312

285863BV00001B/3/P

9 781619 965829